STARS, GALAXIES, and the MILKY WAY

CRABTREE
Publishing Company
www.crabtreebooks.com

Crabtree Publishing Company
www.crabtreebooks.com
1-800-387-7650

Published in Canada
Crabtree Publishing
616 Welland Avenue
St. Catharines, ON
L2M 5V6

Published in the United States
Crabtree Publishing
PMB 59051
350 Fifth Ave, 59th Floor
New York, NY 10118

Author: Clive Gifford
Editorial director: Kathy Middleton
Editors: Izzi Howell, Shirley Duke
Designer: Clare Nicholas
Cover design and concept: Lisa Peacock
Proofreaders: Kathy Middleton
Prepress technician: Ken Wright
Print and production coordinator: Margaret Amy Salter

Published by Crabtree Publishing Company in 2016

The website addresses (URLs) included in this book were valid at the time of going to press. However, it is possible that contents or addresses may have changed since the publication of this book. No responsibility for any such changes can be accepted by either the author or the Publisher.

Printed in the USA/082015/SN20150529

Picture credits:
Shutterstock/A-R-T cover (background), Shutterstock/notkoo cover (tl), Dreamstime/Goinyk Volodymyr cover (tc), NASA, Jeff Hester, and Paul Scowen (Arizona State University) cover (bl), Shutterstock/Petrafler cover (bl), Shutterstock/Vadim Sadovski cover (br), Shutterstock/A-R-T title page (background), Shutterstock/solarseven title page (bc).
Shutterstock/vit-plus 4 (background), Shutterstock/Lorelyn Medina 4 (bl), Shutterstock/fad82 4 (bl), ESA/NASA/Hubble 4 (br), NASA/JPL-Caltech 5 (tr), Shutterstock/RedKoala 5 (br), Shutterstock/RedKoala 6 (bl), Science Photo Library/Lionel Bret/Look At Sciences 7, Shutterstock/Catmando 8 (l), Shutterstock/andromina 8 (bc), Stefan Chabluk 9, Science Photo Library/Mark Garlick 10 (tl), Shutterstock/Happy Art 10 (bl), Shutterstock/gornjak 11 (bl), ESA/Hubble & NASA 11 (tr), NASA, ESA, and JPL-Caltech 11 (br), NASA/Penn State University 12 (tl), NASA/CXC/JPL-Caltech/STScI 12 (bl), ESA/Akira Fujii 13, NASA/Rogelio Bernal Andreo (Deep Sky Colors) 14 (tr), Science Photo Library/Christian Darkin 14 (bc), Shutterstock/bioraven 15 (tr), Wikimedia/Sephirohq 15 (br), Wikimedia/Antonello Zito 16 (bl), NASA/Dana Berry, Sky Works Digital 16 (tr), Thinkstock/lilipom 17 (bl), NASA/ESA/Hubble Heritage (STScI/AURA)-Hubble/Europe Collab. 17 (tr), Shutterstock/bioraven 17 (br), Shutterstock/sciencepics 18-19, ESO 20-21 (c), Shutterstock/Skocko 21 (tr), Shutterstock/Lorelyn Medina 21 (br), NASA/Dana Berry 22 (tl), Shutterstock/RainsGraphics 22 (bl), Shutterstock/vector illustration 23 (bl), Wikimedia/Mysid/Jm smits 23 (tr), X-ray: NASA/CXC/SAO; Optical: Detlef Hartmann; Infrared: NASA/JPL-Caltech 24, NASA/JPL-Caltech/STScI/Vassar 25 (bc), Shutterstock/Malinovskaya Yulia 25 (tr), X-ray - NASA / CXC / Caltech / P.Ogle et al., Optical - NASA/STScI, IR - NASA/JPL-Caltech, Radio - NSF/NRAO/VLA 26 (bl), Shutterstock/RedKoala 26 (br), NASA/JPL-Caltech 27, NASA/ JPL 28, Shutterstock/Viktar Malyshchyts 29 (tc), Shutterstock/fattoboi83 29 (tr), Shutterstock/andromina 29 (br).

Design elements throughout: Shutterstock/PinkPueblo, Shutterstock/topform, Shutterstock/Nikiteev_Konstantin, Shutterstock/Vadim Sadovski, Shutterstock/ CPdesign, Shutterstock/Elinalee, Shutterstock/Hilch.

Library and Archives Canada Cataloguing in Publication

Gifford, Clive, author
    Stars, galaxies, and the Milky Way / Clive Gifford.

(Watch this space!)
Includes index.
Issued in print and electronic formats.
ISBN 978-0-7787-2022-5 (bound).--ISBN 978-0-7787-2026-3 (pbk.).--
ISBN 978-1-4271-1689-5 (pdf).--ISBN 978-1-4271-1685-7 (html)

    1. Stars--Juvenile literature. 2. Sun--Juvenile literature.
3. Galaxies--Juvenile literature. 4. Milky Way--Juvenile literature.
I. Title.

QB801.7.G54 2015   j523.8   C2015-903179-6
                                          C2015-903180-X

Library of Congress Cataloging-in-Publication Data

Gifford, Clive, author.
    Stars, galaxies, and the Milky Way / Clive Gifford.
        pages cm. -- (Watch this space!)
    "First published in 2015 by Wayland"
    Includes index.
    ISBN 978-0-7787-2022-5 (reinforced library binding : alk. paper) --
    ISBN 978-0-7787-2026-3 (pbk. : alk. paper) --
    ISBN 978-1-4271-1689-5 (electronic pdf : alk. paper) --
    ISBN 978-1-4271-1685-7 (electronic html : alk. paper)
    1. Stars--Juvenile literature. 2. Galaxies--Juvenile literature. 3. Milky Way--Juvenile literature. I. Title.

QB801.7.G54 2016
523.8--dc23
                                          2015015360

CONTENTS

STARRY SKIES................................4

OUR NEAREST STAR................................6

A PROTOSTAR IS BORN................................8

MAIN SEQUENCE STARS................................10

SEEING STARS................................12

STAR QUALITY................................14

STRANGE STARS................................16

STAR DEATH................................18

SUPERNOVA!................................20

NEUTRON STARS AND PULSARS................22

GALAXIES................................24

GALAXY TYPES................................26

THE MILKY WAY................................28

GLOSSARY................................30

FURTHER INFORMATION................................31

INDEX................................32

STARRY SKIES

Distant stars and planets both look like small pinpricks of light, but they are quite different bodies. Planets shine in the night sky because their surfaces reflect light from another source. Stars are the real deal—they shine by producing their own light.

What Is A Star?

A star is a massive sphere of gases held together by **gravity**. Stars give off large amounts of heat and light energy. This energy is generated in the core, or center, of the star.

FAMILIES OF STARS

Galaxies are enormous collections of stars, planets, and clouds of dust and gas, all kept together by gravity. Gravity is the force of attraction between objects. Our galaxy is called the Milky Way. Its neighbors include the Large Magellanic Cloud and the mighty Andromeda Galaxy.

Twinkle, twinkle, little star, how I wonder what you are?

Well, it's a giant ball of gas, mostly hydrogen, held together by its own gravity.

The mysterious Large Magellanic Cloud

Long Light

The distances between objects in space are MASSIVE, far too large to measure in miles or kilometers. Astronomers measure distances in space in **light-years**. A light-year is the distance light travels in an entire year. Considering that light covers a whopping 983,571,000 feet (299,792,458 m) in a single second, a light-year is a really long, long way—588,000,000,000 miles (9,461,000,000,000 km).

The stunning Andromeda Galaxy

HELLO NEIGHBORS!

The Canis Major Dwarf is one of the closest galaxies to Earth—only 25,000 light-years away. The Andromeda Galaxy is also thought of as a neighbor, yet it is over two million light-years away.

HOW MANY STARS ARE THERE?

No one is totally sure. The National Aeronautics and Space Administration (NASA) estimates that there are hundreds of billions of stars in the Milky Way alone. Multiply that by the number of other galaxies in the universe and you get an unbelievably HUGE number.

4.24

= THE DISTANCE IN LIGHT-YEARS FROM EARTH TO PROXIMA CENTAURI, THE NEAREST STAR OUTSIDE OUR SOLAR SYSTEM

OUR NEAREST STAR

Big enough to fit 103 million Earths inside it, the Sun is a mere 93 million miles (149.6 million km) from our planet. That may sound like a huge distance to us, but it's close enough for astronomers to study it in detail.

CORE POWER!

The high temperature and pressure in the Sun's core cause the nuclei, or the center of **atoms**, in hydrogen gas to join together to form the gas helium. This process is called **nuclear fusion**. It generates huge amounts of heat and light energy.

LONG JOURNEY

Energy from the core travels in waves through the Sun's **radiation** zone, or the layer around the core. This journey may take as long as 100,000 years. The energy then moves through the next layer, called the convection zone, on swirling currents of hot gas before reaching the star's surface.

62,137 (100,000)

= THE HEIGHT IN MILES (KM) OF LARGE CLOUDS OF HOT GAS THAT SHOOT FROM THE SUN, MORE THAN 11,000 TIMES THE HEIGHT OF MOUNT EVEREST

WHAT IS THE SUN MADE OF?

The Sun is made up of around 74% hydrogen, 25% helium, and small amounts of other elements.

The Sun's outer **atmosphere**, or corona, stretches out over a few million miles (several million kilometers). Some parts reach temperatures of 3,600,032°F (2,000,000°C).

Rising and falling currents in the convection zone carry energy to the surface.

Solar prominences are large clouds of hot gas that occasionally shoot up from the Sun's surface.

Sunspots are part of the Sun's surface that appear darker because they are cooler than the surrounding areas.

Inside the Sun

The **dense** radiation zone surrounds the core.

The core of the Sun is phenomenally hot at about 27 million°F (15 million°C).

The Sun's surface, or photosphere, is made up of hot gases having an average temperature of 9,932°F (5,500°C).

Above the photosphere is the chromosphere, the Sun's 1,243-mile- (2,000 km) thick inner atmosphere.

A PROTOSTAR IS BORN

Stars are born in giant clouds called stellar nebulae. **These provide us with some of the most breathtaking sights found in the universe. Recently-formed stars are known as protostars.**

Clouding Around

Stellar nebulae are formed from gas and dust. These clouds can be far larger than our entire solar system, which is one to three light-years wide. The Thor's Helmet Nebula measures over 30 light-years across.

Pillars of Creation

EAGLE EYES

The Eagle Nebula is around 6,000 light-years from Earth. Spectacular images of it have been captured by the Hubble Space Telescope. Within the nebula, there are columns of gas and dust reaching an astounding 23 trillion miles (37 trillion km) high. Astronomers call these the Pillars of Creation.

800,000
= THE ESTIMATED NUMBER OF STARS AND PROTOSTARS FOUND IN THE TARANTULA NEBULA

The Start Of A Star

1

Most nebulae remain inactive until they are disturbed by a collision between galaxies, a star passing nearby, or a supernova explosion. A supernova is when a star explodes and ejects most of its **mass** so that it flares much brighter all of a sudden.

2

These disturbances push and pull at the nebula. Gravity causes parts of the cloud to collapse in on itself.

3

As the cloud collapses, it begins to spin, causing more and more gas and dust to clump together. Over time, the center gets denser and heats up, creating a protostar.

MAIN SEQUENCE STARS

As a protostar grows, its core becomes denser and hotter. At around 18 million °F (10 million °C), a protostar's core may ignite and start turning hydrogen into helium. This process, called nuclear fusion, generates monstrous amounts of energy.

Hydrogen is converted to helium in a nuclear fusion reaction.

In Sequence

Once a star is carrying out nuclear fusion, it is said to be in its **main sequence**. Most stars spend the majority of their life as a main sequence star, only changing when they run out of hydrogen as fuel. The Sun is roughly halfway through its main sequence, which will last 9 to 10 billion years. Most of the stars we can observe in space are in their main sequence.

40 BILLION (36 BILLION)
= THE APPROXIMATE AMOUNT OF HYDROGEN, IN TONS (METRIC TONS), THE SUN USES AS FUEL EVERY MINUTE. DON'T WORRY! IT HAS ENOUGH TO CONTINUE TO BURN FOR BILLIONS OF YEARS.

Pressure vs. Gravity

Two competing forces, pressure and gravity, stop main sequence stars from changing shape or size. Gravity pulls gas in toward the center of the star, while pressure from the star's core pushes outward.

Proxima Centauri is a main sequence star. Although it is the nearest star to our solar system, it is not visible to the naked eye because it isn't very bright.

FAILED STARS

Smaller protostars, with less than one tenth of the Sun's mass, never become real stars. They don't have enough mass to carry out nuclear fusion, so they exist as warm bodies in space called brown dwarfs. They tend to be between 10 and 80 times the size of Jupiter.

Discovered in 2014, WISE 0855–0714 is the coolest brown dwarf known, with a temperature of -54.4 to 8.6°F (-4 to -13°C) Chilly!

This illustration shows what a brown dwarf might look like.

SEEING STARS

Up to 6,000 stars can be seen from Earth with the naked eye. Telescopes and other instruments have revealed many millions more.

Super-Close Stars

About a dozen stars are less than 10 light-years away from us. The number of stars increases farther out. Between 10 and 50 light-years away, there are 2,000 known stars.

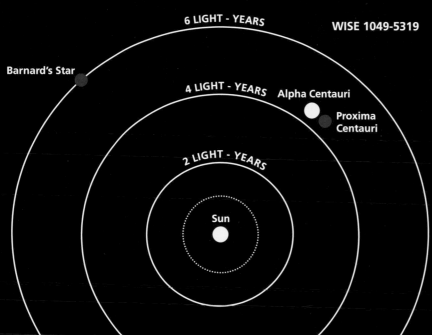

WISE 0855-0714

6 LIGHT - YEARS

WISE 1049-5319

Barnard's Star

4 LIGHT - YEARS   Alpha Centauri

Proxima Centauri

2 LIGHT - YEARS

Sun

Stars seem to twinkle in the Small Magellanic Cloud.

WHY DO STARS TWINKLE?

Actually, most stars don't twinkle. It is Earth's moving atmosphere that causes the light from a star to bend, giving the impression of flickering.

Traveling In Time

Powerful telescopes can peer deep into the night sky and spot dimmer and more distant stars. The farther away a star is, the longer it takes for its light to travel through space to reach Earth. This means that if astronomers view a star 1,000 light-years away, they are actually viewing what it looked like 1,000 years ago. Awesome!

SEEING FAR

Some stars can be seen clearly in the night sky despite being extremely distant. Rho Cassiopeiae is a giant star around 8,200 light-years from Earth. Yet, because it shines much more brightly than the Sun, it can be viewed from the northern hemisphere of Earth without a telescope.

APPARENTLY...

Apparent magnitude is a measure of how bright a star is when viewed from Earth. The lower the magnitude, the brighter the star. The brightest star from Earth is the Sun at -26.74 magnitude, followed by Sirius at -1.46 magnitude.

Night sky

Procyon
(magnitude 0.38)

Betelgeuse
(magnitude 0.5)

Sirius
(magnitude -1.46)

STAR QUALITY

Not all stars look the same. Stars vary greatly in size, color, temperature, and brightness.

Hot Stuff!

The Sun is far from the hottest star around. Some stars have a surface temperature over six times hotter than the Sun. Delta Circini, for example, is a star with a surface temperature of around 63,000°F (35,000°C). What a scorcher!

Rigel, a star with a whopping 62 million-mile- (100 million km) **diameter**, casts its blue-white light over the Witch Head Nebula.

Witch Head Nebula

SPECTRAL TYPES

Astronomers group stars into classes, called spectral types, based on their color and temperature. There are seven main types. The Sun is a type G star.

Spectral Type	Color	Temperature °F (°C)	Star Examples
O	Blue	>54,000°F (>30,000°C)	Delta Circini, Sigma Orionis
B	Blue-white	17,582–54,032°F (9,750–30,000°C)	Z Canis Majoris, Rigel
A	White	12,812–17,582°F (7,100–9,750°C)	Sirius A, Vega, Fomalhaut B
F	Yellow-white	10,652–12,812°F (5,900–7,100°C)	Canopus, Wasp-24
G	Yellowish	9,392–10,652°F. (5,200–5,900°C)	The Sun, Alpha Centauri
K	Orange	7,052–9,392°F. (3,900–5,200°C)	Pollux, Gliese 86, Arcturus
M	Reddish	3,632–7,052°F. (2,000–3,900°C)	Antares, Proxima Centauri

O   B   A   F   G K M

RED DWARFS

The smallest stars that fuse hydrogen are known as red dwarfs. More than half of the stars in the universe may be red dwarfs, including our nearest star, Proxima Centauri. As a result, they may last a thousand billion years before their hydrogen is used up. They will then collapse inward under their own weight and become white dwarfs. Scientists theorize they may eventually turn into black dwarfs, but none exist yet that we can see.

20
= THE NUMBER OF SECONDS IT TAKES THE PISTOL STAR, A SPECTRAL TYPE B STAR, TO GIVE OFF THE SAME AMOUNT OF ENERGY AS THE SUN DOES IN A YEAR.

Mu Cephei was nicknamed the Garnet Star for its deep red color. It is one of the most luminous stars, around 350,000 times brighter than the Sun.

Bright Lights

Luminosity is a measure of how much energy a star gives off. Think of it as how brightly a star shines. A star that shines more brightly than others in the night sky is either closer to us or has greater luminosity than the others. Rigel is over 800 light-years away, but it is the seventh-brightest star that people can see from Earth because of its intense luminosity—117,000 times stronger than the Sun's.

STRANGE STARS

Some stars hang around in pairs, steal gas and dust from other stars, or vary how brightly they shine. Meet some of the strangest stars in space.

Paired Up

Binary stars are pairs of stars that are bound together by one another's gravity. The two stars **orbit** the center point of their mass. The star Sirius, perceived by the naked eye as one single star, is actually a binary star pair, made up of Sirius A and B.

These two white-dwarf binary stars are locked in an orbit that shrinks by one inch (2.5 cm) per hour. Scientists estimate that they will merge in a few hundred thousand years.

STELLAR STEAL

Some binary stars interact with each other. One star pulls **matter** from the other star. The matter either makes the star swell in size or forms a disk, called an accretion disk, around the star.

Stolen matter from the larger star is forming an accretion disk around the smaller star.

accretion disk

On And Off

Cepheid **variable** stars change their brightness over regular periods, for example, every six weeks in the case of RS Puppis. The changes in the light caused by the swelling and shrinking of this variable star helped scientists accurately calculate the star as being 6,500 light-years from Earth, with a 1% margin of error.

The variable star RS Puppis is 200 times larger and 15,000 times brighter than the Sun.

STAR SYSTEMS

Some stars aren't just part of a pair, they are part of a star system containing three, four, or more stars all bound together by gravity. Algol, for example, is a star system made up of three stars. Every 68 hours, the orbits in which two of these stars move causes one to eclipse the other, blocking it out when viewed from Earth.

Off You Go!

The force of gravity between the four stars in the T Tauri star system has recently caused its smallest member—about one fifth the size of the Sun—to be flung out of the system!

100–1,000

= THE NUMBER OF SECONDS IT TAKES ZZ CETI VARIABLE STARS TO CHANGE BRIGHTNESS. THAT IS FAST IN ASTRONOMY!

STAR DEATH

Stars don't exist forever. When a star runs out of hydrogen gas, it can no longer create nuclear fusion reactions at its core. This is called reaching the end of its main sequence. What happens in the star's final stage depends on its size and mass.

Sun-sized star

RED GIANTS

If a star is about the size of the Sun, it will continue to generate nuclear fusion with the hydrogen from its outer layers. This causes its core to shrink and its outer layers to expand. The star swells in size becoming what is called a red giant.

SUPERGIANTS

If a star is much bigger than the Sun, it will follow the same process to become a red giant. This red giant continues to grow until it becomes a red supergiant.

massive star

COLORFUL CLOUDS

As the red giant runs out of fuel, its core collapses, forming a **planetary nebula**. This doesn't mean it has planets. The star's outer layers are flung away, creating a ring-shaped shell of gas clouds.

WHITE DWARFS

When the clouds of the planetary nebula break up, the core of the former red dwarf remains. Now called a white dwarf, this small, dense body cools over billions of years.

red giant

planetary nebula

white dwarf

red supergiant

Type II supernova

neutron star

EXPLOSIVE END

When a supergiant runs out of fuel, it explodes. Called a Type II supernova, it will go on to become a very dense neutron star (see page 22) or a **black hole**.

black hole

SUPERNOVA!

A supernova is a giant explosion that rips a star apart. These star deaths are among the most violent events that happen anywhere in the universe.

Types Ia And II

Supernovae occur in different ways. A Type Ia supernova occurs when matter is transferred between two binary stars. A Type II supernova occurs when a large star runs out of hydrogen fuel, swells to become a supergiant, and starts fusing heavier and heavier elements in its core. Eventually, the core cannot support its own mass and starts collapsing in on itself rapidly.

EXPLOSIVE EVENTS

As the star's core collapses dramatically, energy causes an ENORMOUS shock wave to rebound outward, blowing away the outer layers of the star with tremendous force and speed. Astronomers measured debris from the 1987A supernova and found it hurtling away at speeds of 19 million mph (30 million km/h)!

HOW HOT IS A SUPERNOVA?

The surface of a supernova may reach 360,032°F (200,000°C), but at its core, temperatures may soar as high as 180 billion°F (100 billion°C). This creates vast amounts of light energy. Some supernovae may shine more brightly than an entire galaxy.

Scientists imagine that a Type Ia supernova looks something like this.

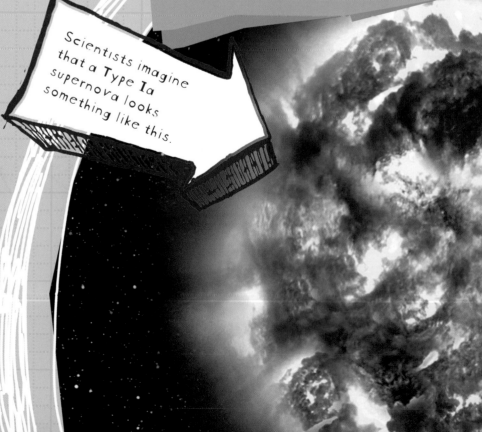

Daytime Viewing

The last major supernova in the Milky Way seen from Earth was Kepler's Supernova, named after the famous German astronomer Johannes Kepler. He was able to view it in 1604 with the naked eye even though it was located 20,000 light-years away. This supernova was so bright that for three weeks it could be seen during the day from Earth.

10 BILLION
= THE NUMBER OF TIMES BRIGHTER THAN THE SUN THAT A SUPERNOVA MAY SHINE AS IT EXPLODES

ANCIENT REMAINS

The remains of a supernova can provide long-lasting viewing for astronomers. In 1054 CE, Chinese astronomers spotted a star in the night sky that was bright enough to be observed for the following two years. Scientists believe this was a giant supernova whose remains formed the Crab Nebula, which is studied by astronomers to this day.

Young Guns

In 2011, 10-year-old Canadian schoolgirl Kathryn Aurora Gray discovered a new supernova—Supernova 2010lt—while studying photos taken by a powerful telescope at Abbey Ridge in Canada. Two years later, her brother Nathan also discovered a new supernova!

NEUTRON STARS AND PULSARS

A supernova scatters most of a star's material across space, but a small, very heavy core can remain, collapsing in on itself even further to reduce its atoms to neutrons and form a neutron star.

Incredibly Dense

Neutron stars are the densest stars of all. Most measure about 12.4 miles (20 km) in diameter but contain as much matter as the entire solar system. To put it another way, if you could ever grab a spoonful of neutron star, it would crush the spoon immediately because it would weigh more than 1.1 million tons (1 million metric tons)!

Astronomers have discovered around 2,000 neutron stars in space so far.

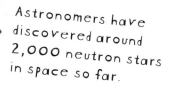

Heavy Stuff
According to scientists, a lump of neutron star the size of a baseball would weigh 22 billion tons (20 billion metric tons)—almost 40 times the weight of all the people on Earth!

A MATTER OF SOME GRAVITY

The mass of the extremely dense neutron stars means they exert an incredible amount of gravity. The gravity you would experience on a particularly dense neutron star could be as much as a trillion times what we experience on Earth.

In A Spin

Discovered in 1967, pulsars are neutron stars that spin and send out regular streams of matter and radiation. The Vela pulsar completes 11 spins every second—faster than a helicopter's blades. It also emits a jet of matter that is almost three quarters of a light-year long.

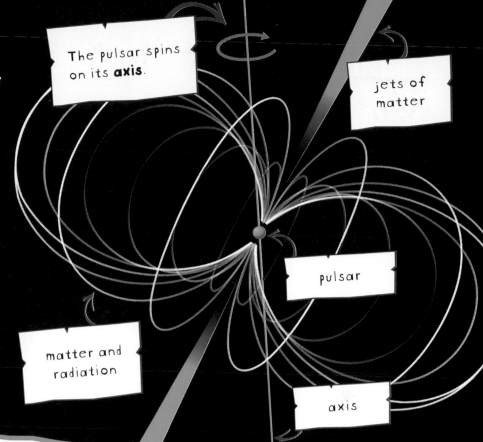

The pulsar spins on its **axis**.

jets of matter

pulsar

matter and radiation

axis

BURSTING WITH ENERGY

A neutron star's intense gravity puts its surface under huge pressure. Sometimes, parts of the surface break, releasing a giant burst of energy called a starquake. One starquake recorded in 2004 lasted just a fraction of a second, but it released an estimated 10,000 trillion trillion trillion watts of energy. Wow!

43,000
= THE NUMBER OF COMPLETE SPINS THE FASTEST KNOWN PULSAR, J1748−2446AD, MAKES EVERY MINUTE

WHAT IS A MAGNETAR?

A magnetar is a neutron star with an incredibly powerful magnetic field, approximately one thousand times stronger than an ordinary neutron star's and hundreds of millions of times stronger than any man-made magnet.

GALAXIES

Galaxies are giant groupings of stars, planets, nebulae, interstellar matter (clouds of gas and dust), and other bodies held together by gravity.

Number Of Stars

The number of stars in a galaxy varies greatly. A small galaxy contains fewer than one billion stars, but some galaxies hold over **400** billion stars. The Andromeda Galaxy is thought to contain as many as a trillion stars!

WHY DO MANY GALAXY NAMES START WITH THE LETTER 'M'?

The M stands for Messier Catalog, a list of galaxies and nebulae put together by the French astronomer Charles Messier and his assistant, Pierre Méchain, in the 18th century.

Astronomers have found over 3,000 regions of the M101 galaxy (also known as the Pinwheel Galaxy) in which new stars are being formed. M101 is about 170,000 light-years wide.

Crash, Bang, Wallop!

Galaxies occasionally collide with one another. These collisions can continue for millions of years. The two colliding Antennae galaxies have been crashing into each other for at least **100** million years. The massive forces created by the collision are helping to trigger the formation of new stars.

103

= THE NUMBER OF OBJECTS, INCLUDING MANY GALAXIES, LISTED IN MESSIER'S FINAL CATALOG PUBLISHED IN THE 1780s. ALL MESSIER OBJECTS CAN BE SPOTTED USING A SMALL TELESCOPE OR GOOD BINOCULARS.

LONG CRUNCH

Another pair of galaxies, NGC 2207 and IC 2163, have just started colliding. Scientists estimate that it will take a billion years for the two galaxies to merge, forming one giant elliptical galaxy.

Some people think that these colliding galaxies look like a mask.

GALAXY TYPES

Galaxies come in many different shapes and sizes. These shapes include elliptical, spiral, barred spiral, lenticular, and irregular.

Old Ovals

Elliptical galaxies have a round or oval shape and tend to contain more old stars and fewer new stars than some other types of galaxy. Astronomers rate these galaxies on their roundness from E0 for a near-perfect ball to E7 for a long, cigar-shaped oval.

The M106 spiral galaxy is moving away from us at a speed of 334 miles per second (537 km/s)— that's 1,201,200 mph (1,933,200 km/h)!

IN A SPIRAL

Spiral galaxies are among the most majestic-looking of all galaxies. Spiral galaxies appear to have a series of long, curving arms packed full of stars, nebulae, and gas when viewed from above or below. Some, like the Sombrero Galaxy, can only be seen sideways from Earth.

5.5 MILLION
= THE ESTIMATED DIAMETER IN LIGHT-YEARS OF THE BIGGEST KNOWN GALAXY, IC1101.

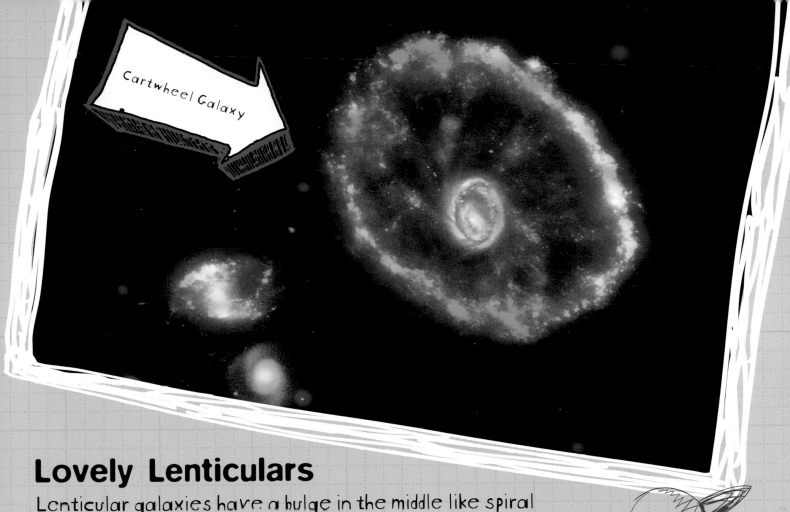

Cartwheel Galaxy

Lovely Lenticulars

Lenticular galaxies have a bulge in the middle like spiral galaxies, but no swirling arms. The Cartwheel Galaxy is an unusual lenticular galaxy. Astronomers believe it was hit by a smaller galaxy around 100 million years ago, and this caused ripples of intense new star formation. These new stars created a ring around the galaxy's center.

WHAT IS A BARRED SPIRAL GALAXY?

Viewed from space, some spiral galaxies have what looks like a solid bulge across their center, made up of gas, dust, and stars. These are known as barred spirals. New stars form at the end of the bar and in the galaxy's arms.

NOT FITTING IN

Some galaxies don't fit in any category. These are called irregular galaxies and may have been caused by collisions or near misses with other galaxies, which pulled them out of shape. The Large Magellanic Cloud, a neighbor of the Milky Way, is an irregular galaxy. It is thought to contain around 10 billion stars.

THE MILKY WAY

The Milky Way is the galaxy we call home. We cannot view the whole galaxy because we're in it, but scientists have figured out that it is a large barred spiral galaxy made up of a somewhat flat disk of stars, gas, and dust. The galaxy has arms spiraling out from the center.

Vital Statistics

The solar system may feel like a pretty big place, but light can travel from the Sun past all the planets in less than a day. In contrast, the Milky Way is ENORMOUS! It takes light over 100,000 years to cross the entire Milky Way.

Scutum-Centaurus Arm

Illustration of what the Milky Way looks like

Sagittarius Arm

Perseus Arm

Sun

Orion Arm

WHAT'S IN THE CENTER OF THE MILKY WAY?

Scientists think there is a supermassive black hole at the heart of our galaxy, which they have named Sagittarius A. Black holes are points in space with so much matter that their gravity is strong enough to pull anything into it, including light.

LOCATION, LOCATION

The solar system isn't slap bang in the middle of things. We are situated about 27,000 light-years from the center of the Milky Way. We are positioned on the Orion arm between two of the galaxy's main spiral arms—Perseus and Sagittarius.

> The Milky Way as we see it from Earth

Long-Distance Trip

The solar system orbits the center of the Milky Way at an extremely rapid speed of 492,126 mph (972,000 km/h), but the vast journey it has to make means that a complete orbit takes around 225 million years.

Galaxy Eater

The Milky Way is a cannibal galaxy. In the past, it has consumed small galaxies drawn in by its gravity. It is currently gobbling up the Canis Major Dwarf Galaxy.

OLD-TIMER

Around 190 light-years from us, in the Milky Way, is the oldest known star in the entire universe. HD 140283, also known as the Methuselah star, is estimated to be at least 13.2 billion years old, almost as old as the universe itself!

100 BILLION
= THE MINIMUM NUMBER OF STARS IN THE MILKY WAY

GLOSSARY

apparent magnitude A measurement of how bright a star is when viewed from Earth

atmosphere The gases surrounding the surface of a planet

atom The basic unit of matter

axis An imaginary line that goes through the center of an object that is spinning

black hole An object in space with such strong gravity that nothing nearby can escape its pull, including light

dense (density) A measure of how much matter an object contains. A very dense object has a lot of matter in a small space.

diameter The distance across the middle of a circle, or through the middle of a sphere

gravity The invisible force of attraction between objects

light-year The distance traveled by light in a year

main sequence The period when a star carries out nuclear fusion

mass The amount of material an object contains

matter Physical things that take up space such as solids, liquids or gases

nebula/nebulae (pl.) A cloud of dust and gas in outer space

neutron A particle in an atom's nucleus with no electric charge

nuclear fusion The process inside a star that joins the centers of hydrogen atoms together to form helium, generating energy

orbit To travel around another object in space in an elliptical path

planetary nebula A nebula in a ring shape formed by a shell of gas around a star that is aging

radiation Different kinds of energy from heat or light

stellar nebula A cloud of dust and gas from which stars are formed

variable Changes taking place over a period of time

FURTHER INFORMATION

Books

Space Travel Guides: The Sun and Stars
by Giles Sparrow (Smart Apple Media, 2012)

The Stars: Glowing Spheres in the Sky
by David Jefferis (Crabtree Publishing Co., 2009)

The Sun: A Super Star
by Chaya Glaser (Bearport, 2015)

Websites

http://science.nationalgeographic.com/science/
space/universe/galaxies-article/
Galaxies, their formation, and kind

www.nasa.gov/vision/universe/solarsystem/sun_
for_kids_main.html
The importance of the Sun and top 10 Sun facts

www.lpi.usra.edu/education/skytellers/galaxies/
about.shtml
Pictures and facts about different types of galaxies.

INDEX

Andromeda Galaxy 4, 5, 24

apparent magnitude 13

binary stars 16, 20
black dwarf 15
black hole 19, 28
brown dwarf 11

Canis Major Dwarf 5, 29
cepheid variable stars 17

Eagle Nebula 8
Earth 5, 6, 8, 12, 13, 15, 17, 21, 22, 26, 29

galaxies 4, 5, 20, 24, 25, 26, 27, 29
collision between 9, 25, 27
definition of 4
types of 26-27

Large Magellanic Cloud 4, 27
light-year 5, 8, 12, 13, 15, 17, 21, 23, 29, 26, 28, 29
luminosity 15

magnetar 23
main sequence stars 10-11
Milky Way 4, 5, 21, 27, 28, 29

neutron star 19, 22, 23
nuclear fusion 6, 10, 11, 18, 22

planetary nebula 19
protostar 8, 9, 10, 11
Proxima Centauri 5, 11, 12, 14, 15
pulsar 22, 23

red dwarf 15, 19
red giant 18, 19
red supergiant 18, 19,
Rigel 14, 15

Sirius 13, 14, 16
Small Magellanic Cloud 12
spectral types 14
star
death 18, 20
definition of 4
density
formation 8, 9, 25,
nearby 12
starquake 23
stellar nebula 8
Sun 6, 7, 10, 11, 12, 13, 14, 15, 17, 18, 21, 28
sunspot 7
supernova 9, 19, 20, 21, 22

white dwarf 15, 16, 1